I am not just pretty;

I am _____ too.

Daniellie Marie

I Am Not Just Pretty; I Am _____ Too.
Copyright © 2019 Daniellie Marie

All rights reserved. No part of this book may be copied or reproduced in any form without written permission from the publisher.

Illustrator: Edward Davis III, Triumph Multimedia LLC

Cover design and layout: Yvonne Smith, Light and Virtue LLC

ISBN: 978-1-937400-97-2

Printed in the United States of America

PeeWee Press; A Division of Manifold Grace Publishing House, LLC.
Southfield, Michigan 48033
www.manifoldgracepublishinghouse.com

DEDICATION

To my nieces Vannessa and Janessa,

Your beauty radiates and permeates to everyone who knows you. Your lives shine so brightly, we all need a pair of sunglasses when we're around you. Vannessa, your kindness is breathtaking, your humor is absolutely contagious and your strength is amazing. Janessa, your loyalty is incomparable, your drive is admirable and your confidence is simply undeniable.

I am beyond proud of you ladies. I love you!

ACKNOWLEDGMENTS

A special thanks to Relounna and Rykeil Wright, who inspired me to write this book because of their love for reading. You girls are so amazing and I pray God continues to bless you both beyond your wildest dreams. Don't stop believing, and never stop reading.

MESSAGE FROM A DAD

Daniellie Marie has given the world one of the most creative and incisive books for young girls that I have ever come across. In a culture that is transfixed on marginalizing, objectifying, and certainly celebrating women based on their physical features, *"I am not just pretty; I am _____ too"* proves to be a counter cultural breath of fresh air. Daniellie focuses her lens on the beauty that lives within as she encourages these young girls to recognize their value beyond their physical attributes, uncovering the non-physical aspects of their beauty.

As beings made in the image of God, we come in a variety of skin tones, hair textures, and body types. We are distinct in our gifts and interests, but each of us has been entrusted with His communicable attributes, such as: love, self-awareness, justice, grace, and mercy. Daniellie Marie masterfully provokes thought to help girls all over the world become acquainted with the person God has uniquely created them to be. She lovingly appeals to young girls encouraging them to activate God's love in their relationships and interactions.

As a father of three, this book is an awesome supplement to bible reading and teaching in our home where we strive to teach our daughters, (and our son) to live lives of integrity and godly character. I warmly commend this compelling journey for girls of all ages.

You are not your body. You are not your experience. You are not your function/job/activity. You are not just pretty, you are made in the image of God and that is the basis of your significance and purpose.

- Dr. Leython H. Williams, Sr.

HEY PRETTY GIRL,

This book is really special to me and I am super excited to share it with you!

Being pretty isn't just about how we look, the length of our hair, the color of our skin or the types of clothes we wear. This is why I can call you a pretty girl without even looking at you. Being pretty is a reflection of who we are and how we treat others.

I've invited some of my friends to be a part of this book and help me share with you. They have been the best friends a girl could ever ask for, and I am so thankful for them. They encourage me and they lovingly correct me when I am not being so pretty.

As you read this book, I hope you will become more aware of your character and the beauty that comes from within. Character is what makes you more than just pretty.

When you see throughout the book, this will be your chance to interact and share with an adult you trust. Let's make reading and learning FUN!

Pretty Girl, Pretty Girl, let's explore your pretty world.

When you hear the word '*pretty*', what is the first thing you think?

 If you're like me, your first thought might be, something you can physically see.

If I said, 'pretty girl', who is the first person that comes to mind? *Why?*

Did you think of yourself? Because you are absolutely a pretty girl!
You're not just *pretty*; you're *amazing* too!

To me, being pretty is not just about how you look. It's not just about what you wear, your body type, the color of your skin or the length and texture of your hair.

Being pretty is so much more than what you can see.

When people tell me I am pretty I say, "Thank you!"
I even believe it's true, but I am not just pretty.
I have other amazing attributes too.

*An attribute can be defined as a quality, feature or characteristic of someone or something. *

In your own words, what is an **attribute**?

_____

_____

_____

_____

_____

What are some of your positive attributes and character traits?

1._____ 2._____ 3._____

Ok, let's add to your list of attributes. Feel free to say, *"**Me too**"* when we get to a character trait that describes you.

 I am not just pretty; I am <u>INQUISITIVE</u> too.

I value wisdom and having an understanding, so I am not afraid to ask questions when things are unclear to me. Knowledge is powerful, and I am empowered by truth.

I am not just pretty; I am <u>SMART</u> too.

I love to learn! I enjoy reading, math and writing. Yes, I am a pretty girl who likes going to school!

I am not just pretty; I am <u>UNIQUE</u> too.

I recognize I don't have to compete with anyone else, because God created me just the way He wanted me to be. There is no one in the world who is exactly like me (even if I had a twin), and that makes me special and unique.

# I am not just pretty; I am <u>COMPASSIONATE</u> too.

We never know what someone is going through, so I think it is important to give compassion and love freely. It doesn't cost a thing to listen without judgment, forgive quickly, and help those who are in need.

I am not just pretty; I am <u>UNDERSTANDING</u> too.

Sometimes things happen that we can't control, but instead of getting mad, we should try to see things from other's point of view and consider how they might feel too.

I am not just pretty; I am <u>HONEST</u> too.

Honesty begins with me, and being honest with myself gives me the freedom to grow. When I look in the mirror, I want to see all there is to know. I cannot work on improving me, if there are things I refuse to see.

I am not just pretty; I am <u>FUNNY</u> too.

Making people laugh is something I love to do. They say I am funny by the things I say and naturally do.

I am not just pretty; I am <u>OPTIMISTIC</u> too.

Having a positive perspective isn't always easy. Especially when things happen unexpectedly, but I try to look for the good in every situation and encourage others to do the same.

I am not just pretty; I am <u>AUTHENTIC</u> too.

Being authentic means staying true to who God has created me to be, despite my own insecurities and people's opinions of me. When I look at me, I love the girl I see.

I am not just pretty; I am <u>NICE</u> too.

I am helpful and really like doing kind things for others, especially when they don't expect it and didn't ask me to.

I am not just pretty; I am <u>FORGIVING</u> too.

Forgiveness allows me to live freely and without resentment. We are human and we are going to make mistakes; this is why God gives us grace. It's important to forgive others when they've wronged us. We must ask for forgiveness when we hurt others and forgive ourselves when we've made a bad choice.

Are you mad at someone because of something they said or did? Is someone upset with you because of something you did or said? If yes, talk to an adult about the situation and ask them for advice on forgiveness.

 I am not just pretty; I am <u>DETERMINED</u> too.

I am determined to always grow, become a better person, reach my goals, then set new ones.

Alisha

 I am not just pretty; I am <u>PATIENT</u> too.

I am learning to wait until it is my turn, without getting an attitude. Besides, what will getting upset actually do? It won't make me get what I am waiting for any faster!

I am not just pretty; I am <u>POLITE</u> too.

I think it is important to say things like, "may I, please, excuse me, and thank you." It is also polite to refer to adults by the name they prefer.

 *Ask an adult to let you know when you're being polite this week, so you can become more aware of it.*

I am not just pretty; I am a <u>VISIONARY</u> too.

I am committed to the vision and goals I have for my life. I am confident that I can accomplish anything if I am willing to work hard for it.

I am not just pretty; I am __GRATEFUL__ too.

Each day is a gift, and when we receive gifts, we should be thankful and express our gratitude by saying, "thank you". Let's take a minute to list a few things we are thankful for today.

1. _____   2. _____   3. _____

I am not just pretty: I am a __PROBLEM SOLVER__ too.

When we're faced with a challenging situation, we may not know exactly what to do; but thinking through things critically is necessary to figure out the best solution. Of course, you should always talk to an adult when you have a problem, so they can help you.

I am not just pretty; I am <u>TENACIOUS</u> too.

When I decide to accomplish something, I'm not easily derailed.

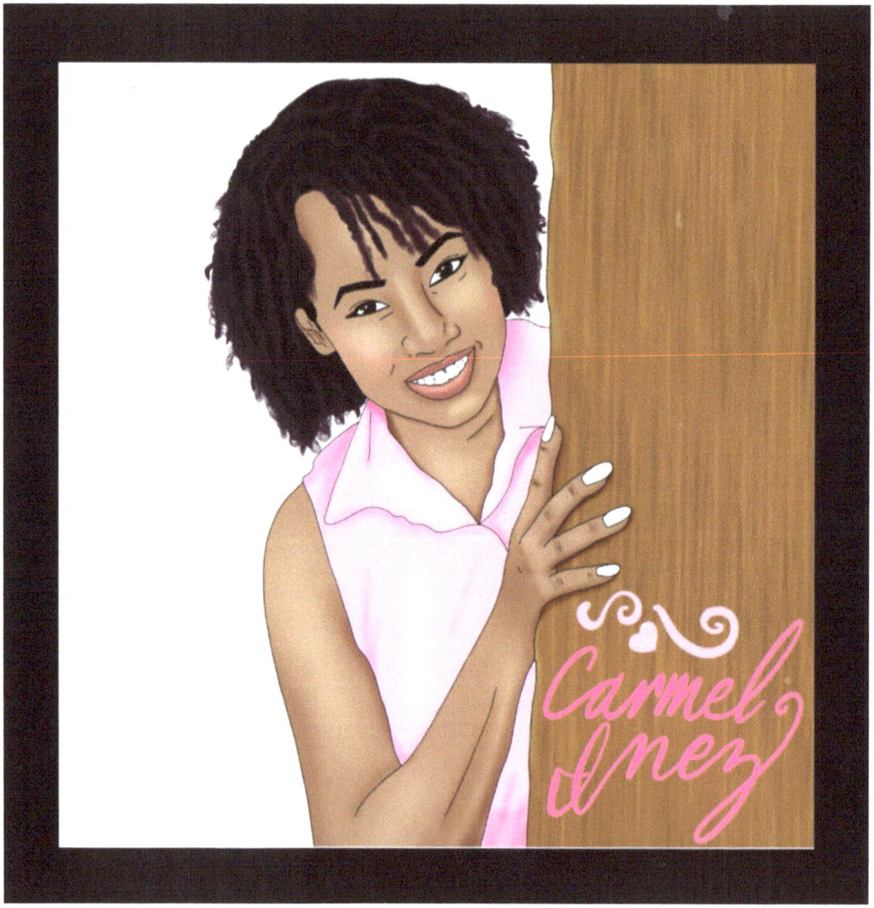

I am not just pretty; I am <u>TALENTED</u> too.

I am dedicated, committed and hardworking. When I stay focused, I can be and do anything. I can be an actress, an artist, an author and an athlete.

What are some of your talents?

1. _____
2. _____
3. _____

I am not just pretty; I am FREE too.

I am naturally free to be me! I don't allow the opinions of others to define or control me. Financial freedom is also very important to me. It allows me to give and live freely.

I am not just pretty; I am <u>TRUSTWORTHY</u> too.

When I say things, people believe I am telling the truth. When you're honest, people know you have integrity and will know you are trustworthy.

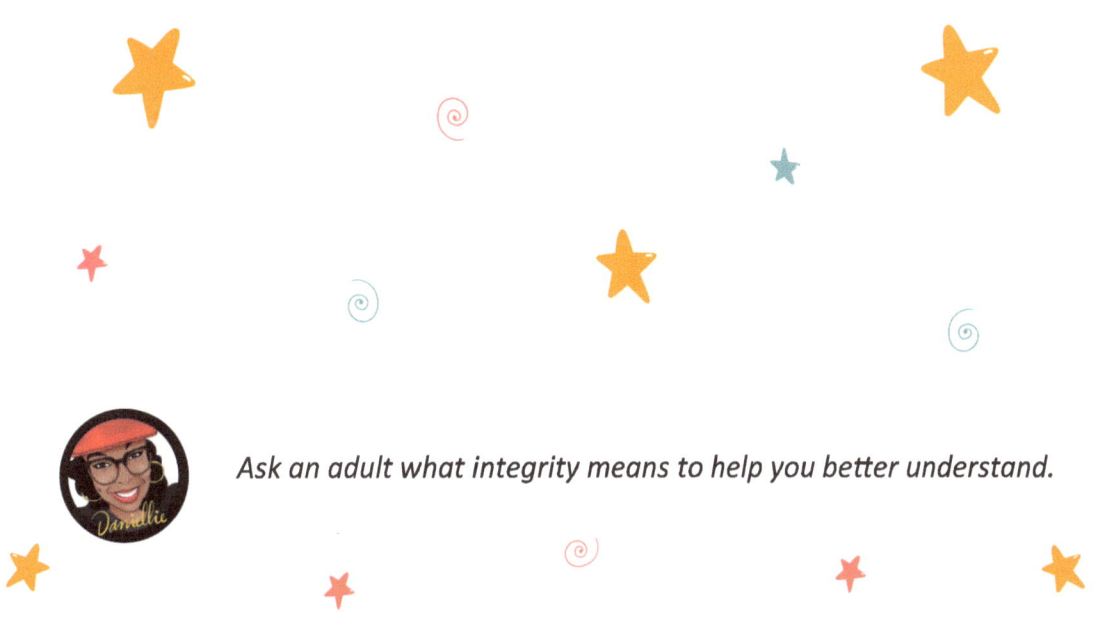

Ask an adult what integrity means to help you better understand.

I am not just pretty; I am <u>HARDWORKING</u> too.

I give 100% to everything I do and when I commit to any project, my team knows I am going to come through. When I choose to take on a task, I work diligently until it is completed to the best of my abilities.

I am not just pretty; I am <u>RELIABLE</u> too.

My friends know they can count on me to do the things I said I would do. Even when I am faced with a challenge, I figure out a way to get it done, because I am a problem solver too.

I am not just pretty; I am <u>GENEROUS</u> too.

Generosity isn't limited to giving money. There are many ways we can help make our world and our community a better place. You can volunteer your time, share your talents and even donate money to charities.

 *Ask an adult to help you identify a need in your community, then think of ways you can be generous by giving.*

I am not just pretty; I am <u>FEARLESS</u> too.

Fearlessness is a state of mind that propels you to embrace destiny, maturity, and be accepting of others. I am proud to be fearless.

I am not just pretty; I am <u>ADVENTUROUS</u> too.

I enjoy trying new things with friends and family to create memories. Some adventurous things might include horseback riding, camping, kayaking, traveling, and even sightseeing. I wonder what cool things you and your family will do?!

I am not just pretty; I am <u>PECULIAR</u> too.

I embrace the things that make me different. I own the things that made me unique. I don't have to fit in with the crowd because I am simply me!

I am not just pretty; I am HAPPY too.

My joy comes from within, so I am happy no matter what is happening. Of course, there are other emotions I feel too, because I am human just like you. No matter what's going on, there is so much to be grateful for and thinking of these things always makes me happy.

Select an adult you trust, and talk to them about your feelings because they are important. If there is something happening that makes you unhappy, please share that too, so they can help you. There are many people who love and care about you.

I am not just pretty; I am <u>INTELLIGENT</u> too.

I believe having a quality education gives us the tools to succeed.

I am not just pretty; I am ENERGETIC too.

Some people say I am the life of the party, and I guess it's kind of true. I just love bringing energy to everything I do.

I am not just pretty; I am FUN too.

I love to hang out with my friends, laughing, talking, sharing, eating, and taking a lot of pictures to capture those moments forever.

I am not just pretty; I am <u>MODEST</u> too.

While friends, magazines, and social media tell me that I must wear certain types of clothing to be accepted, I have decided to be a trendsetter. I can be fashionable without compromising on the cut of my shirt or the length of my skirt. Modesty is my favorite outfit!

I am not just pretty; I am <u>HUMBLE</u> too.

There are things that I do well, and areas that I can improve in. Being humble is accepting my gifts and struggles, knowing that my value in God is greater than my performance!

I am not just pretty; I am <u>WISE</u> too.

Using wisdom helps us make good choices in any situation. It's the ability to know what to say and do; and what not to say and not to do. Many times, we respond without even thinking and later realize the choice we made wasn't the best decision. When we slow down to think of the consequences of our decisions, usually we choose wisely.

I am not just pretty; I am <u>RESILIENT</u> too.

I can't wear my strength on my face, but it is in my spirit. It is in my ability to endure life's setbacks, detours, tragedies, disappointments and bounce back. Resilience is my super power.

I am not just pretty; I am QUIET too.

Just because I am quiet doesn't mean there is something wrong. Sometimes I enjoy doing things alone like: listening to music, reading a book, drawing, writing or just relaxing.

Are there times when you feel like you need quiet time? Talk to an adult about this, and what this special quiet time does for you. Some of us girls really do need time to help us shine.

I am not just pretty; I am <u>STRONG</u> too.

Throughout life there will be challenges, but I refuse give up. I am a survivor and more than a conqueror.

I am not just pretty; I am <u>ACCEPTING</u> too.

I can hang around with many different types of people and embrace the beauty of our differences. I want people to feel they can be themselves around me.

I am not just pretty; I am <u>FRIENDLY</u> too.

I can make friends easily, everywhere I go. At school I meet new friends by simply smiling and saying, "Hello".

I am not just pretty; I am <u>CREATIVE</u> too.

I am constantly changing, evolving and realizing it is okay to be more than just one thing. I have lots of ideas and enjoy creating new things.

I am not just pretty; I am <u>PERSISTENT</u> too.

I won't give up on my dreams, even when they seem too big for me. I believe if I keep working towards it, I can do anything I put my mind to. I will keep trying until I reach my goal.

What goals have you set for yourself?

_____, _____ ,_____.
_____, _____ , _____.

Now, envision yourself reaching these goals. If you can believe it, then you can achieve it!

Congratulations in advance!!!

HEY PRETTY GIRL,

Our story time has come to an end, but the good news is you can read it again. You can even read the book with friends. I wanted to give you an opportunity to be a part of the story by adding your photo and personal attribute on the next page.

Name:

_____

I am not just pretty; I am _____ *too.*

Give a brief description of your attribute:

_____

_____

_____

_____

ABOUT THE AUTHOR

Growing up, Daniellie Marie associated being "pretty" with a certain look. She often heard people complimenting girls on their skin tone, the length/texture of their hair and the stylish clothes they'd wear. While she was frequently celebrated for her academic achievements and leadership skills, being told she was "pretty" was rare. That is until she became an adult at which time people seemed to take more notice of her physical appearance, yet diminished the attributes that truly made her beautiful. A professional man once told her he couldn't believe how smart she was because she was "so pretty". An elderly woman shared with her, how surprised she was to have met a young lady who was pretty and nice. As if being both were unfamiliar to her.

Comments such as these inspired Daniellie Marie to tell a different story. She wrote this book to address the stereotypes that have subconsciously been placed on girls of all ages. She hopes the next time you see a beautiful girl you'll take a deeper look at her, and see beyond what you can physically see, because she is more than just pretty.

Daniellie Marie is a singer/songwriter, author, speaker and a girl who loves God. Daniellie graduated from Central Michigan University with her Bachelor of Science degree in Psychology and graduated from Wayne State University with her Master of Social Work degree. She is a clinical social worker and a certified prevention specialist with the Michigan Board of Addiction Professionals. She currently serves as a rehabilitation specialist and business consultant.

Daniellie Marie is also the author of *My Heart; My Responsibility: A Single Woman's Guide to Waiting*. She is the executive producer of her gospel EP, *Led by Love*. She is the host of Moments with Daniellie Marie, the Podcast and the founder and owner of We Talk, LLC.

Connect with Daniellie:
To request Daniellie Marie for speaking engagements, book readings and bulk book purchases, please visit: www.danielliemarie.com

Email: wetalk@danielliemarie.com

Social Media: *Instagram:* @daniellie_marie

Facebook: Facebook.com/wetalk.danielliemarie